# We...
# Country
# Cooking

**A selection of traditional and well-loved recipes**

## Chris Grant

Cover illustration:
Allan Grant

Gwasg Carreg Gwalch

First edition: 1993
Revised edition: 2008
© Text: Chris Grant

ISBN: 978-1-84527-207-4

Published by Gwasg Carreg Gwalch
12 Iard yr Orsaf, Llanrwst, Wales LL26 0EH
📞 01492 642031   📠 01492 641502
✉ books@carreg-gwalch.co.uk
Web site: www.carreg-gwalch.co.uk

# WELSH COUNTRY COOKING

# CONTENTS

# PREFACE

Cookery is an act of love. These recipes were regularly made by my mother's grandmother and great grandmother and they represent a happy and secure Welsh childhood. Some of them are quite well known, others less familiar, but all of them rekindle fond memories — frosty days and warm fires, summer walks and picnics on the beach — a time when life moved at a slower and more satisfying pace, when pleasures were discovered in simple things.

May this book always bring you delight in the taste of home-cooked and wholesome food.

# NOTE

In the case of some recipes, I only know their Welsh names, some are known by both their Welsh and English names, and those originating in the Southern and Eastern anglicised areas of the country have only English names.

# INTRODUCTION

This book contains many old and traditional Welsh recipes, but it also includes recipes in regular use in Welsh households from the Victorian period to the present time. Some are just well loved Welsh family recipes of uncertain age.

A little historical background is provided to show how recipes were born and developed and how the Welsh climate and landscape have contributed to the choice of ingredients.

Many of these tasty old recipes are now finding their way into restaurant menus as we try to recapture that 'essence of Welsh spirit' which reflected the warmth and hospitality of the Welsh hearth and home in days gone by.

# LEEK RECIPES

The leek (and also the daffodil) were adopted widely as Welsh emblems during the holocaust of the Wars of the Roses in the fifteenth century: The coat of arms of Henry Tudor (later to become King Henry VII of England) were green and white, so his Welsh followers were said to have adopted the emblems of the leek and the daffodil with their symbolic greenish white stems.

Leeks are also, incidentally, one of the few cultivated vegetables mentioned by name in the laws of the tenth century Welsh Prince Hywel Dda. Another theory about the leek as a national emblem of Wales developed out of the general belief that St David the Welsh patron saint was able miraculously to survive on a diet of leeks and water. It is also part of the folklore of Wales, that a leek was worn as a national identification badge by the Welsh troops who defeated the Saxons at the Battle of Heathfield in 633.

At a time when the Christian religious festival of Lent was important, meat could not be eaten and leeks provided an useful and sustaining form of vitamins. Thus leeks were particularly valuable in the spring and early summer. Leeks grow very well in Welsh soil benefitting from a more than ample rainfall and are found in an amazing variety of recipes. Here are just a few traditional ones:

# CREAM OF LEEK SOUP

2oz (50g) of butter
1¼lb. (575g) leeks, trimmed and washed carefully
2 large onions finely chopped
3 sticks of celery including leaves
Tablespoon of chopped parsley
1 large potato, chopped and peeled
2½ pints (1.4 litres) chicken stock
Salt, white pepper to taste
¼ pint (150ml) cream

Heat the butter in a sturdy pan. Chop the leeks roughly. Put the leeks into the pan together with the celery. Cook slowly for 10-15 minutes on a gentle heat. Add the potato and stir to absorb the butter. Add the parsley, stir in the stock and seasoning, slowly bringing the mixture to the boil. Simmer for about half and hour until the vegetables have softened.

Put the mixture through a fine sieve or liquidiser and transfer to a clean pan. Add the cream and reheat gently.

# LEEK BROTH
# CAWL CENNIN

A medium sized piece of salty bacon
Potatoes
Carrots
Leeks
Parsley
Cabbage
(Use as many of the following as you can spare, or sufficient for a meal)

Place bacon in boiling water with the carrots and potatoes. After boiling these together for about an hour and a half, add the leeks and some shredded white cabbage with a spoonful of chopped parsley. This traditional 'cawl' can be thickened by adding two tablespoons of oatmeal turned into a paste with cold water.

In poorer Welsh households, the broth would be drunk as the first course of a meal and the meat and vegetables kept back as the main course. Sometimes the leftovers were retained for the following day's breakfast fare.

## LEEK PASTY

*¾lb (350g) flour*
*6oz (175g) lard*
*Pinch of salt, teaspoon baking powder*

*Oven setting — Gas Mark 6 — 400°F*

Rub the above mixture together well with cold water into a dough. Cut into two and roll out thinly to cover a large ovenproof dinner plate. Take about three handfuls of prepared leeks and lay over the first layer of pastry. Next, put a few strips of fat bacon on top of the leeks with salt and pepper. Add an egg-cup of water, then place the next layer of paste on top and cook in a fairly hot oven till done.

# BRAISED LEEKS

*(Sufficient for about 4 people)*
*8 good sized leeks*
*2oz (50g.) butter*
*½ pint chicken stock*
*Salt (preferably seasalt)*
*Black pepper*
*Green peppercorns if available.*

*Preheat oven to Gas Mark 4 (350°F)*

Carefully clean and wash the leeks ensuring there is no dirt in the leaves. Grease an ovenproof dish with some butter and place the whole leeks into it. Bring the chicken stock to the boil, season with salt and pepper and add the butter. Cover and bake in the oven for 40 minutes, removing the lid for the last 5 minutes of cooking time. Garnish with parsley and peppercorns if liked.

This dish was popularly eaten with the Welsh Sunday roast dinner.

# LEEK PIE

*8 leeks washed and cut into small pieces*
*1oz (25g) butter*
*4oz of chopped smoked bacon*
*¼ pint (150ml) of stock*
*Salt and pepper*
*1 bay leaf*
*12oz (350g) shortcrust pastry*
*1 beaten egg*

Heat the butter in a frying pan and add the pieces of bacon which must be fried for about five minutes. Add the leeks and cook together on a gentle heat for around three minutes. Pour in enough stock to cover the leeks, add the bay leaf, season and simmer for about 10-15 minutes. Remove the liquid from the pan and set the remainder aside to cool.

Grease a shallow pie dish with butter, roll out the pastry to about one quarter of an inch (5mm) thickness and cut two circles to line and cover the dish. Line the pastry with one circle of pastry and insert the filling. Cover with the second circle. Make a small steam hole in the top of the pie, press the edges down and brush the top with beaten egg. Bake in the oven for about 30-40 minutes.

This dish is especially tasty in summer when served with grilled tomatoes.

# MEAT DISHES

Chickens when young were a luxury in Wales and were generally roasted as in many other parts of the UK (until the middle of this century and the advent of the frozen creature). Older birds, not suitable for roasting, were, however, turned into tasty hotpots and casseroles.

## WELSH CHICKEN
## FFOWLYN CYMREIG

*1 or 2 chickens*
*½lb (225g) of bacon*
*½lb (225g) of carrots*
*1oz (25g) butter*
*1oz (25g) flour*
*1 small cabbage*
*2 large leeks*
*Mixed herbs*
*Salt and pepper*
*½ pint (300ml) stock*

Dice the bacon, leeks and carrots. Put them into a casserole with the butter and fry for a few minutes, stir in the flour until it thickens and browns. Place the whole chicken in the sauce, adding the leeks, chopped small cabbage, herbs and seasoning. Add the stock, a knob of butter on top of the bird and simmer for about 2 to 3 hours.

To serve, place the chicken on a bed of the cooked cabbage, pouring the broth on top.

# WELSH CHICKEN HOTPOT

*1 tablespoon of butter (or vegetable oil)*
*4 chicken quarters*
*12oz (350g) leeks*
*12oz (350g) new potatoes scrubbed (Pembrokes if available)*
*½ pint (300ml) dry cider*
*Sprigs of rosemary*
*Salt and pepper*

Heat the oil in a casserole or large saucepan and fry the chicken till browned. Trim and clean the leeks and slice thickly. Add the leeks, potatoes, cider and rosemary to the pan or casserole. Add seasoning and bring to the boil. Cover with a tightly fitting lid and simmer for 40 minutes or until the chicken and vegetables are tender. Serve with cider sauce and vegetables.

It may come as s surprise that lamb — that traditional Welsh delicacy — was not a common meal in Wales until the eighteenth century. Most sheep were kept for wool until that time, the elderly beasts only being served as mutton. In fact, until the eighteenth century with the advent of more efficient farming methods, most animals were killed in the autumn and their meat salted down for the winter. Rich sauces and spices were often used to disguise the salty flavour.

# WELSH LAMB PIE

*1½lbs (700g) of neck of lamb*
*Teaspoonful of finely chopped parsley*
*Bunch of young carrots*
*Salt and pepper*
*Short crust pastry*

*Oven setting — Gas Mark 6 — 400°F*

Bone the meat and cut into small pieces. Clean and cut the carrots into thin slices. Put one layer in the bottom of the dish, then add meat, parsley and seasoning. Repeat this process until all is used; cover with water, until just below the top of your dish. Cover with pastry and brush over with milk. Bake for two hours in a moderate oven.

After 20 minutes' cooking time, turn the oven down to Gas Mark 4 (350°F). The resulting dish is very ancient in origin. It can be served either hot or cold.


# HONEYED LAMB
# CIG OEN A MÊL

This delicious dish contains a number of Welsh specialities: Welsh honey preferably made from wild mountain flowers, and fresh typically Welsh herbs — wild thyme, rosemary and mint.

*4lb (1.8kg) shoulder of Welsh lamb*
*1 clove of garlic*
*Sea salt*
*Freshly ground pepper*
*4oz (125g) honey*
*¾ pint (450ml) dry cider*

*1 teaspoon of chopped mint*
*1½ teaspoons of chopped thyme*
*1oz (25g) plain flour*
*1 teaspoon of lemon juice*

*Oven setting — Gas Mark 8 (450°F)*

Line a roasting dish with a piece of foil which is large enough to wrap over the joint. Rub the meat all over with the clove of garlic. Place the joint in the tin and season well with salt and pepper.

Mix half a pint of cider (300ml) with the honey, and pour over the joint. The mint and thyme should then be carefully sprinkled over the top of the meat. Fold the foil loosely over the meat and cook in the oven for 30 minutes.

At the end of this time, open the foil and baste with the rest of the cider. Then return to the oven, closing up the foil parcel, reducing the oven temperature to (350°F) Gas Mark 4. The dish must be cooked for a further hour, opening the foil for the meat to brown after 30 minutes. Remove the meat and place on serving dish to keep hot.

To make the gravy, pour the meat juices into a saucepan and allow to stand for five minutes and then skim off the surface fat. Blend the flour with 4 tablespoons of the liquid in a basin and stir back into the saucepan. Bring to the boil until smooth and thickened. Add the seasoning and serve with the joint. Baked onions and new minted potatoes are superb as accompaniments to the dish.

# MONMOUTHSHIRE BROTH

*1 Best end of neck of lamb*
*2 large onions*
*1lb (450g) carrots*
*1¼lbs (600g) potatoes*
*Salt and pepper*
*Parsley*

Place the washed meat in a large saucepan of cold water; add the chopped onions and sliced carrots and bring slowly to the boil. Remove any scum and allow meat to simmer for one to two hours. Add potatoes half an hour before the broth is to be served. Add salt and pepper to taste and garnish with fresh chopped parsley.

# SPICED BEEF

*12lb flat ribs*
*¾lb (225g) salt*
*¼lb (112g) of Demerara sugar*
*1oz (25g)saltpetre*
*¼ ounce (6g) pepper*
*¼ ounce (6g) cloves*
*¼ ounce (6g) allspice*
*¼ ounce (6g) mace*

Bone the meat; mix the salt, sugar and other ingredients together. Place the meat in a deep dish and sprinkle over with the dried mixed ingredients. Turn the meat every day for a fortnight (not a recipe for the impatient!). At the end of the fortnight, wash well and roll up and tie. Place in a casserole with some beef dripping and roast in a moderate oven for four hours. Turn out on a meat dish, cover with a plate and place a weight on top. Beef treated in this way becomes very tender and spicy. It is best served cold with salad. It is ideal for lunch on a hot summer's day or as a light supper dish at any time of year.

## WELSH BEEF STEW

*(Quantities are not precise in this very old dish — it all depended on the size of your family!)*

*Beef*
*Potatoes*
*A handful of carrots*
*Onions*
*A small swede*
*Small piece of bacon (if available)*

Slice up the meat into small pieces; place in a saucepan with less cold water than necessary for soup; simmer for about 1 hour before adding carrots, onions, swede (all diced up); continue to simmer for about half an hour. Finally add chopped potatoes and seasoning.

This dish was obviously designed for the old kitchen range and it is essential that it be cooked very slowly, and not allowed to become dry. It is best served with plenty of fresh bread.

## BACON HOTPOT

Fill a casserole with alternate layers of Welsh bacon, sliced onions and thickly sliced potatoes. Add salt and pepper. Cover with a lid and cook slowly for two or three hours. Remove the lid for the last 20 minutes to brown the top. (This would be an useful and warming evening meal to slow cook for working people who can set their oven to automatic.)

*Oven setting — Gas Mark 3 (325°F)*

# RABBIT PIE

*Pastry*
*1 rabbit*
*½lbs (225g) beef steak*
*¼lbs (112g) cooked ham*
*2 teaspoonful chopped parsley*
*Nutmeg*
*Salt and pepper*
*Nutmeg*
*Stock*

Soak the rabbit in salted water for an hour and a half. Joint it and place it in a pie dish with the ham and steak, cut into small pieces; sprinkle with parsley, salt and pepper, and nutmeg. Add the stock and cover with pastry. Bake slowly for an hour and a half.

# FAGGOTS
# FFAGOD SIR BENFRO

*1½lbs (700g) pig's liver*
*4ozs (125g) breadcrumbs*
*3ozs (75g) suet*
*2 large onions*
*1 or 2 teaspoons chopped sage*
*2 teaspoons salt*
*¼ teaspoon pepper*

*Oven setting — Gas Mark 5 (375°F)*

Mince the raw liver and onions into a bowl. Mix with breadcrumbs, suet, salt, pepper and sage thoroughly. Form into small balls. Bake in a moderate oven for about half and hour; add boiling water into the tin to make a tasty gravy.

# STWNS RWDAN A IAU

This is a popular North Wales dish which is very economical.

*Liver*
*Onions*
*Swede*
*Potatoes*

Slice up the liver and fry till dark brown. Dip into seasoned flour. Place the liver and onions into a saucepan or casserole, cover with water and simmer slowly for two or three hours.

Serve with potatoes and swedes well mashed together into what is known as a 'stwns'. Incidentally, mashed potatoes and swede is a delicious alternative to chips and is superb with sausages, bacon, chops etc.

# GLAMORGAN SAUSAGES

*1 egg*
*A little finely chopped onion*
*Pinch of mixed herbs*
*Pinch of mustard*
*salt and pepper*
*5oz (150g) breadcrumbs*
*3oz (75g) grated cheese*

Separate the egg yolk from the white. Mix all the dry ingredients and bind with the egg yolk. Divide into small sausages and roll in flour. Dip each into egg white, then roll in breadcrumbs and fry in pork fat (or lard). Drain on kitchen paper and serve with creamed potatoes or chips.

# CAWL HASLET

*1lb (500g) pig's liver*
*1lb (500g) onions*
*1lb (500g) potatoes*
*Salt and pepper*

Cut liver into small pieces, slice onions and prepare potatoes. Allow the liver and onions to simmer in three pints (1.7lts) of water for one and a half to two hours. Add potatoes, simmer for another half hour, season with salt and pepper. Strain and serve very hot.

# GRANNY'S BROTH
# CAWL MAMGU

*2lb (1000g) best end of neck (Welsh lamb)*
*1 small swede*
*½lb (250g) carrots*
*1lb (500g) potatoes*
*2 large leeks*
*1oz (25g) parsley*
*½oz (12g) flour*
*Salt and pepper*

Place the meat into a saucepan, cover with cold water, add the salt and pepper. Bring slowly to the boil and skim off the fat carefully. Add the carrots sliced in half, sliced swede and the white of the leeks. Simmer gently for 2 to 2½ hours. Add the potatoes (cut into 4) and continue to simmer for another 30 minutes. When the potatoes are almost cooked, thicken with the flour and a little water. Finally, add the green of the leeks and chopped parsley. Simmer for another 10 minutes, and serve in basins while piping hot.

# TREGARON BROTH
# CAWL MAMGU TREGARON

*1½lbs (750g) bacon*
*1lb (500g) shin beef*
*1 white cabbage*
*½lb (250g) carrots*
*½ a small swede*
*½lb (250g) parsnip*
*1lb (500g) potatoes*
*1 large leek*
*Oatmeal to thicken*

Use a large saucepan and ensure all the meat and vegetables are covered by water. Boil the ingredients, except the leek, together and leave to simmer for as long as required. Pop in the leek just 10 minutes before serving and let the 'cawl' boil.

# FISH AND SEAFOOD

Welsh streams and rivers are renowned for their trout and salmon. The seas off the coast of Wales were also once abundant with a variety of seafoods — alas overfishing has reduced seafish, but once they provided a much greater part of the Welsh diet than nowadays.

## SUPPER HERRINGS
## SWPER SGADAN

This recipe is interesting because it reminds us of the simplicity of the old Welsh kitchen. Often its equipment was little more than a griddle, a bakestone and a great iron pot suspended over a fire. In traditional Welsh cooking, boiling and stewing were most commonly used methods of food preparation.

In the rest of the county, for example, herrings would almost always be fried or grilled.

At one time herrings were very plentiful off the Pembrokeshire coast, and when available, are still the best in Wales.

*4 filleted herrings*
*1 tablespoon of prepared mustard*
*Salt and pepper*
*1oz (25g) butter*
*1½lbs (700g) potatoes, peeled and thinly sliced*
*1 large onion*
*1 large cooking apple, cored and sliced*
*¼ teaspoon dried sage*
*2oz (50g) melted butter*

*Oven setting — Gas Mark 4 (350°F)*
Spread the cut side of the herrings with mustard and sprinkle with salt and pepper. Roll them up starting at the tail end. Spread the butter over a pie dish large enough to include all the ingredients.

Line the dish with a layer of sliced potatoes and then a layer of onion and apple. Place the rolled herrings on top and cover them with the rest of the onion and apple, ending with a layer of potato. Pour in enough boiling water to come halfway up the sides of the dish. Add the sage, season with salt and pepper and pour the melted butter over the top.

Cover with foil and bake in the oven for 30 minutes. Remove the foil and increase the oven temperature to Gas Mark 6 (400°F). Check the seasoning by tasting and bake for another 20-30 minutes.

This is a complete meal which is enhanced by a tomato salad accompaniment.

## TROUT WITH BACON
## BRITHYLL A CHIG MOCH

Welsh trout, especially from the cold mountain lakes of North Wales, are among the sweetest tasting in Britain.

This recipe has a close Breton equivalent indicating the Celtic links between the two countries.

Sufficient for 6 people:

*6 trout, each about 6-8oz (127-225g)*
*Salt and pepper*
*12 rashers of smoked fatty bacon*
*1 tablespoon chopped parsley*

*Oven setting — Gas Mark 4 (350°F)*

Clean the trout and season them inside, ensuring that they are kept whole. Trim the rinds from the bacon rashers and place them in a baking dish big enough to hold the fish snugly. Place the fish head to tail on top of the layer of bacon. Season and scatter the top with parsley. If the ends of the rashers overlap, lift them over the fish.

Cover with foil and bake for 20 minutes in a preheated oven.

A lovely summer lunch dish served with salad and creamed or new potatoes.

# COCKLE PIE

Cockles were made popular in the British Isles by the Romans. Colonies of cockles proliferated along the coasts of Wales, particularly in the south and west. Traditionally they are available in Welsh markets — the 'cockle lady' with her gingham-covered cockle basket was always a welcome sight.

Cook two pints (1200ml) of cockles in a cup of water. Line the sides of a pie dish with pastry thickly rolled. Put a layer of cockles in the bottom of the dish. Sprinkle with chopped chives or young spring onions, then a layer of bacon which has been diced. Repeat these layers until the dish is full. Pour in liquid in which the cockles were boiled, adding some pepper. With strips of pastry make a criss-cross over the pie. Cook slowly until the pastry is brown.

Oven setting — Gas Mark 6 (400°F)

This is delicious served hot with new Welsh potatoes or cold with a mixed salad.

There is a variation on this dish. You can use sweet corn with the cockles and top with a cheese pastry, or grate some cheese over your shortcrust pastry.


## COCKLE CAKE
## TEISEN GOCOS

Take your cockles and stand them overnight in water sprinkled with oatmeal. Wash well and boil. dip in thick batter and fry a spoonful at a time in hot fat. Very tasty with summer salads.

# LIMPET PIE

*Any quantity of ready cooked limpets*
*¼lb fat or streaky bacon*
*2 hard boiled eggs*
*1 onion*
*Bread dough or short pastry mix*

*Oven setting — Gas mark 7 (425°F) Gas Mark 5 (375°F)*

Line deep pie dish with thinly rolled out dough or pastry. Fill the dish with alternate layers of limpets, cubed bacon, sliced eggs and sliced onion. Add seasoning and a little of the limpet liquid. Cover with dough or pastry. Bake in hot oven for half and hour, and then more slowly for another half hour.

# LAVER BREAD
# BARA LAWR

Laver is an edible seaweed which can be bought already prepared in Swansea Market and elsewhere along the south and west coast of Wales. Some more enlightened fishmongers may also stock it.

To prepare your seaweed, wash it to remove sand and boil for several hours until quite soft. (Once prepared, it can be stored in a freezer, or sterilised screw-top jar for about 1 week for use as needed.) Mix with fine oatmeal and form into small cakes. When fried, preferably in bacon fat, these form part of a traditional Welsh breakfast and are very tasty. Usually they are served with bacon or mixed grills.

When cooking laverbread, the tradition is not to use an iron pan or metal spoon, but wooden spoons and an aluminium saucepan.

Laverbread can also be fried in butter, with a squeeze of lemon and served on hot buttered toast. Another tradition is to add the juice of two seville oranges to the laverbread and serve as an accompaniment to Welsh lamb.

In Cornwall, incidentally, the custom is to eat laverbread cold with vinegar.


## TEIFI SALMON SAUCE

(The Teifi is a river in West Wales).

Wash the salmon in salted water, dry it carefully and cut into slices. Mix three quarters of a pint of melted butter with a glass of port, a little ketchup and one boned anchovy, in a pan over a low flame. Pour this sauce over the salmon, place fish in a covered dish in a moderate oven, leaving it to bake for about three quarters of an hour. (Oven setting Gas Mark 5 375°F).

# POTATO RECIPES

## POTEN BEN FEDI

*2lb (500g) potatoes*
*1 cup minced cooked meat*
*1 rasher bacon*
*1 onion*
*Knob of margarine*
*Tablespoon of flour*

*Oven setting — Gas Mark 6 (400°F)*

Boil potatoes, then mash, adding the knob of margarine and a spoonful of flour. Chop up rasher of bacon and onion and fry them, then add bacon, onion and minced meat to the mashed potatoes.

Add salt and pepper, then mix all together and turn into a greased pie dish and bake in a moderate oven for about 20 mintues until the top is golden brown.

# TEISEN DATWS

Potato cakes were very popular in North Wales during the Victorian period.

*1lb (450g) cold cooked potatoes*
*3 tablespoons flour*
*2 tablespoons brown sugar*
*1 teaspoon baking powder*
*1/4 teaspoon cinnamon*
*Milk to mix to a stiff consistency*

*Oven setting — Gas Mark 7 (425°F) reducing to Gas Mark 4 (350°F)*

Put mixture into a greased tin, and place into fairly hot oven to begin with, then lower the temperature, and leave the cake to bake for two hours.

The cake can be eaten hot or cold, sliced and buttered.

# POTATO CAKES (2)

*1lb (450g) boiled potatoes*
*4ozs (112g) flour*
*1 teaspoon baking powder*
*1 egg*
*1oz (25g) butter or margarine*
*1 tablespoon sugar*
*Pinch salt*

*Oven set to Gas Mark 7 (425°F)*

Melt the butter and mix in all the ingredients. Roll out about one inch thick. Bake either on a griddle or in a hot oven for 20 minutes.

## ONION CAKE
## TEISEN NIONOD

Peel and slice some potatoes and place them in a layer on the bottom of a well buttered cake tin. Sprinkle a layer of finely chopped onion on the potatoes and small lumps of butter or margarine. Repeat these two layers until the tin is full, adding salt and pepper to taste. The final layer must be of potatoes on which some butter is spread. Cover with a lid or plate and bake for one hour in a moderate oven. This cake is traditionally eaten with hot or cold meat. (Oven set to Gas Mark 5 (375°F)

## CARDIGAN CAKES
## TOCYN Y CARDI

*1 tablespoon each of rolled oats and plain white flour*
*2 teaspoons milk*
*1 teaspoon baking powder*
*Pinch of salt*

Mix all the dry ingredients together. Make into small cakes and fry in some bacon fat. Served with fried bacon for a hearty cooked breakfast or supper.

# CHEESE AND EGG DISHES

Cheese making in Celtic cultures dates from very ancient times. It may possibly have been discovered when milk curd was found in the stomachs of young animals being slaughtered. The natural stomach rennet separated the milk into curds and whey.

Huge quantities of cheese were eaten in the Tudor period, and from that time onwards, its popularity was such that many Welsh farmhouses developed their own unique recipes. Wales' own Caerphilly cheese is ideally lightly pressed, containing more water and less fat than, say Cheddar, for example. it has a distinctively mild flavour which is exceptionally delicious with fruits or grilled.

Eggs were always popular, but in the past, the Welsh were equally at home eating seagull, goose, duck and plovers' eggs as much as hens' eggs. In the early middle ages, eggs were most often baked in the fire ashes rather than boiled.

## WELSH RAREBIT
## CAWS POBI

*4oz (100g) grated cheese*
*3 tablespoons milk*
*1oz (25g) butter*
*Salt and pepper*
*Pinch of mustard if liked*
*Slice of toast*

Place the cheese and milk in a saucepan and melt slowly. Add seasoning and butter. When piping hot pour it over the toast and brown under the grill. A little beer is traditionally added to the mixture. A more up-market and slightly luxurious version of this dish includes Stilton Cheese and two teaspoons of red wine.

Very early Welsh recipes for this dish include a layer of cold roast beef, spread with mustard and horseradish beneath the cheese which is then sprinkled with ale and shallot vinegar.

# EGG WHEY
# MAIDD YR IÂR

*Thick slice of bread*
*1-2 eggs*
*½ pint (300ml) milk*
*Ginger, nutmeg and sugar to taste*

Break up the bread into a saucepan. Add the beaten eggs and milk, then the ginger, nutmeg and sugar. Allow to stand on top of the stove until it sets, but do not let the mixture boil. You might prefer to use a cool oven, as for egg custard.


# CHEESE MUFFINS

*1½ cupfuls plain flour*
*½ cupful of grated cheese*
*¼ teaspoon salt*
*4 teaspoons baking powder*
*1 egg*
*¾ cupful milk*

*Oven setting — Gas Mark 7 (425°F)*

Beat the egg lightly and add the salt and milk. Then sift the flour and baking powder together and include the grated cheese. Make into a dough using the milk and then roll out.

Cut into rounds, brush with the beaten egg and bake for 10 minutes in a hot oven.

These are delightful split, spread with butter and eaten hot or cold. (They are nicer hot!)

# CHEESE AND ONION TART

This is another of those trusty lunchpack recipes — it is equally delicious hot or cold. Many a farmer or miner would have enjoyed one of these for his lunch. It is equally useful for picnics or as a supper-time snack.

*Line a tart plate with shortcrust pastry. Fill with the following mixture:*

*2oz (50g) grated cheese*
*1 large tomato*
*1 onion, minced or chopped*
*1 tablespoon cooked potato*
*Salt and pepper to taste*
*2 or more beaten eggs*

*Oven setting — Gas Mark 4 (350°F)*

Line a tart plate with shortcrust pastry and add the above mixture. Bake for about half an hour.

# PUDDINGS

Although in Wales puddings and cakes were enjoyed from mediaeval times, it was not until the seventeenth century with the advent of cheap and easily obtainable sugar that tarts and fruit pies became generally popular. It may now amuse us to learn that in the middle ages, the eating of raw fruit was regarded as harmful to health. Welsh cookery employs a high proportion of dried fruit which saw people through the long winter and spring when little fresh fruit was available.

## SUNDAY RICE PUDDING
## PWDIN REIS DYDD SUL

Boil 1½ozs (35g) of rice in about ½ pint (300ml) milk, and 1oz (25g) sugar with two beaten eggs and add to the boiled rice. Pour the mixture into a pie dish lined with puff pastry. Bake for about half an hour till the custard is set and the pastry browned. (Oven setting Gas Mark 6 (400°F).

# PWDIN REIS MAMGU

*2ozs (50g) rice*
*2ozs (50g) demerara sugar*
*Pinch salt*
*½ pint (300ml) water*
*1 pint milk*
*½ teaspoonful nutmeg*
*1oz (25g) butter*
*1 or 2 eggs*

This is a slightly richer version of the everyday rice pudding. The recipe originates from Caernarfonshire.

Simmer rice in water until grains are swollen. Add butter, sugar and milk, nutmeg and pinch of salt, and cook gently for about two hours, stirring from time to time. Remove from the heat and beat in the egg yolks. Just before serving add stiffly beaten whites of eggs. This is traditionally served with jam or honey.

# PWDIN WATKIN WYNNE

The Wynne family held a position of power in North Wales over the centuries. This must have been one of their favourites.

*10oz (250g) breadcrumbs*
*8oz (225g) chopped suet*
*3oz (75g) sugar*
*3 eggs*
*Pinch of salt*
*Juice and grated rind of two lemons*

Mix well and put into a basin. Cover and boil for three hours. It should then be served with this sauce:

Melt some butter with brown sugar adding grated lemon peel, nutmeg and a glass of sherry or Madeira. Heat this well, but do not allow to boil and serve at once. If you prefer substitute half a wineglass of lemon juice for the sherry if preferred and make up the balance with golden syrup.

## SNOWDON PUDDING
## PWDIN ERYRI

Named after Wales' highest mountain, whose summit is famous for being snow covered until the late days of spring.

*4oz (100-125g) stoned raisins*
*8oz (225g) shredded suet*
*1½oz (40g) plain flour*
*6oz (175g) brown sugar*
*8oz (225g) white breadcrumbs*
*6oz (175g) lemon marmalade*
*Grated rind of 2 lemons*
*¼ teaspoon salt*
*6 eggs, beaten*

*Sauce (Snow on the mountain):-*
*1½oz (40g) caster sugar*
*Rind of half a lemon, whole*
*¼ pint (150ml) water*
*1oz (25g) butter*
*2 level teaspoons plain flour or cornflour*
*4 fl oz (100-125ml) white wine*

Put aside about one handful to the raisins, then mix the rest together with the suet, flour, brown sugar, breadcrumbs, marmalade, grated lemon rind and salt. Beat the eggs and stir into the mixture. Sprinkle the raisins you set aside over the bottom of a large greased basin and pour the pudding mixture on top of them.

Prepare the pudding for steaming, cover with a lid and boil for 3 hours, topping up with boiling water from time to time.

For the sauce, boil the sugar and lemon rind in the quarter of a pint (150ml) of water for about 15 minutes, then discard the rind and add the butter. Take the pan off the heat, and cool it for 10-15 minutes, then stir in the flour to make a smooth mixture. Work in the wine, return the pan to the stove and stir over a gentle heat until the sauce thickens.

Serve this pudding piping hot. Pour the sauce over the pudding shortly before taking it to the table.


## OATMEAL PANCAKES
## CREMPOG GEIRCH

*6oz fine oatmeal*
*1lb plain flour*
*½oz (12g approx.) yeast mixed in a little warm milk*
*and a little sugar*

Mix the two flours, and add the yeast and enough milk to make a thin batter. Cook as pancakes and eat hot, spread with butter or jam.


## PIKELETS
## PICE'R PREGETHWR

*4oz (125g) plain flour*
*2 eggs*
*3oz (75g) butter or margarine*
*½ pint (300ml) milk or buttermilk*

Rub the butter into the flour, beat the eggs and mix into a batter, beating well with a wooden spoon. Allow to stand overnight if possible. Bake on a griddle or sturdy frying pan and eat hot and buttered.

# CREMPOG

This ancient Welsh dish may be based on the old Anglo Saxon 'Crumpet'. It has had a firm place in Welsh tradition over many centuries. Certainly during the early years of present century it was the custom for the children to march singing through the streets. When they returned home they received delicious crempogs usually spread well with butter and black treacle.

Earliest batters were made with water, because it was felt that milk could produce a tough and sticky result. By the eighteenth century, though, most Welsh recipes called for milk and cream.

There are a number of variations on this recipe: for example it can be served with sweet or savoury fillings.

*1oz (25g) butter*
*8oz (225g) plain flour*
*½ pint (300ml) buttermilk (or full cream milk)*
*1 beaten egg*
*½ teaspoon lemon juice*

*Fillings:*
*Jam, fresh fruit such as strawberries, raspberries or blackberries or lemon juice.*
*Savoury ideas: Chopped parsley and shallot*
*(Crempog las) with bacon and fried tomatoes*

Rub the butter into the siften flour and stir in the milk. Whisk in the egg and allow the batter to stand for at least 1 hour. Just before cooking mix the bicarbonate of soda with the lemon juice and beat into the batter.

Heat a greased frying pan about 8 inches (20cm) in diameter and wait for the fat to smoke, put a small quantity of about 3 tablespoons into the pan and allow to cook for about 1 minute either side.

When the pancakes are ready, pile them on to a hot plate, sandwiching the layers together with jam, lemon juice, fruit etc. Cut the warm crempog into quarters to serve.

## APPLE PUDDING
## PWDIN AFAL

*2oz (50g) plain flour*
*1oz (25g) sugar*
*1½oz (38g approx.) butter*
*2 eggs*
*½ pint (275-300ml) milk*
*Stewed apples*
*Vanilla essence*

*Oven control Gas Mark 6 (400°F)*

Melt butter in a saucepan, stir in the flour and add the milk a little at a time. Bring to the boil to make a smooth sauce. Pour into a bowl and add the sugar, a few drops of vanilla essence and the egg yolks. Fold in the beaten egg whites.

Grease a pie dish and cover the bottom with a layer of stewed apples. Pour the mixture over them and bake for three quarters of an hour.

# CAKES

Cakes developed from enriched breads popular with the Romans. But recipes for cakes as we know them rarely appear before the seventeenth century. As ovens became more common and efficient, the baking of richer mixtures became possible. Seed cakes were amongst the earliest raised cakes (an old Welsh seed cake recipe has been included), and during the eighteenth century, fruit and eggs were frequent additions. Wales is renowned for its excellent range of sweet breads and tea-loaves.

## BARA BRITH
## SPECKLED BREAD

This old recipe is believed to be associated with North Wales, but similar loaves were baked all over the country.

Bara Brith was originally made for special events such as Christmas, Harvest time and Eastertime. This particular recipe gives a rich fruity mixture beneath a firm and tasty crust.

*10oz (275g) strong white flour*
*1 level teaspoon salt*
*3⁄4oz (20g) lard*
*1oz (25g) sugar*
*1⁄2 teaspoon mixed spice*
*1 large beaten egg*
*1⁄4 pint (150ml) warm water*
*3⁄4oz (20g) fresh yeast*
*8oz (225g) currants*
*4oz (125g) sultanas*
*1oz (25g) chopped dried peel*

*Oven setting: Gas mark 4 (350°F)*

Sieve the flour and salt into large mixing bowl. Rub in the lard and make a well in the centre. Mix the sugar and spice together and put into the well.

Add the beaten egg to the warm water and use three tablespoons of it to mix the yeast into a smooth thinnish paste, then stir in the rest of the liquid. Pour over the sugar in the well, mix thoroughly to blend then knead well to make a smooth elastic dough. Mix the currants, sultanas and peel together and knead lightly into the dough.

Make the dough into a round or oblong shape, as you prefer and place on a greased baking sheet or in a greased loaf tin. Cover with greased polythene and put in a warm place to rise for 1½ hours.

Bake in a preheated oven for 35 minutes.

## WELSH GINGERBREAD

*¾lb (350g) flour*
*½ teaspoon bicarbonate of soda*
*1 teaspoon cream of tartar*
*6oz (175g) demerara sugar*
*4oz (125g) butter*
*2oz candied peel*
*6oz (175g) black treacle slightly warmed and mixed with a ¼ pint (150ml) milk*
*1 or 2 teaspoons of ground ginger*

*Oven control: Gas Mark 3 (325°F)*

Add the bicarbonate of soda, ginger and cream of tartar to the sifted flour. Rub butter into the flour and add the sugar and peel, mix with the treacle and milk. Bake in a greased tin for 1½ hours.

This was sometimes made for sale at the old Welsh Fairs by omitting the ginger — the flavour of the treacle being a good substitute.

## SEED LOAF
## BARA CARAWE

*1lb (450g) self raising flour*
*1 teaspoon salt*
*1/2 tablespoon carraway seeds*
*1oz (25g) sugar*
*2 1/2oz (65g) margarine or butter*
*1 egg*
*1/4 pint (150ml) milk or milk and water*

*Oven setting: Gas Mark 5 (375°F)*

Sieve the flour and salt into a basin. Rub in the fat and add the other dry ingredients. Mix to a soft dough with beaten egg and milk. Put into a greased bread tin and bake for 1 hour.


## GINGER CAKE
## TEISEN SINSIR

*4oz (125g) butter*
*1lb (450g) plain flour*
*2oz (50g) brown sugar*
*1oz (25g) candied peel*
*1oz (25g) ground ginger*
*2 eggs*
*1 teaspoon of bicarbonate of soda*
*1 teacup of milk*

*Oven control: Gas Mark 4 (350°F)*

Heat together the treacle, butter and sugar. Mince the peel and add the beaten eggs. Put the dry ingredients in a bowl and add the beaten eggs gradually, followed by the treacle, milk etc. as required. Pour into a shallow tin, well greased, and bake for three quarters of an hour.

## CINNAMON CAKE

*½lb (225g) plain flour*
*4oz (125g) sugar*
*4oz (125g) butter*
*Yolk of 1 egg and the whites of 2*
*Half a teaspoon of baking powder*
*1 teaspoon of cinnamon*
*Jam*

*Oven setting: Gas Mark 6 (400°F)*
*(for the meringue, turn down to Gas Mark 3 (325°F)*

Add the baking powder to the flour and rub in the butter. Add the sugar and cinnamon with the yolk of the egg to make a stiff paste. Roll out and place on a shallow tin or plate — as for making a plate tart. Cook 'blind' in a hot oven. Allow to cool and spread with jam. Beat the whites of egg until stiff, fold in a little sugar, spread on top of the jam and return to a cool oven to set.

# ANGLESEY CAKE
# TEISEN SIR FÔN

During the eighteenth century, when this cake originated, treacle was often used in Wales in place of sugar as a sweetening agent — mainly because it was cheaper. It was also used to sweeten other dishes such as porridge and puddings.

Anglesey cakes were popular at weddings of the poorer people who could not afford proper wedding cake. This is a lovely moist dark coloured delicacy.

There were a number of local versions, and some family recipes were handed down from generation to generation.

*Oven setting: Gas Mark 4 (350°F)*

*4oz (125g) margarine*
*3oz (75g) soft brown sugar*
*1 egg*
*10oz (275g) self raising flour*
*1 tablespoon of black treacle*
*¼ teaspoon salt*
*1 teaspoon ground ginger*
*1 teaspoon ground mixed spice*
*½ teaspoon bicarbonate of soda*
*7fl. oz (200ml) milk*
*6oz (175g) mixed raisins and currants*

Cream the fat and sugar till pale and fluffy. Beat in the egg and treacle. Sieve together the flour, mixed spice, salt, and ginger and stir them into the creamed mixture. Dissolve the bicarbonate of soda in the milk, add gradually to the mixture and stir thoroughly before adding the dried fruit. Spoon the mixture into a greased and lined 7-8 inch (18-20cm) cake tin and bake in the preheated oven for 50 to 60 minutes.

The cake tastes nicer if kept for one day before serving.

# ANGLESEY CAKE (2)

3 teacups of plain flour
1 teacup of butter
1 teacup of sugar
3 teaspoons baking powder
2 eggs
Milk to mix
A little dried fruit

*Oven setting: Gas Mark 5 (375°F)*

Rub the butter into the flour, add sugar, baking powder and beaten eggs and milk if necessary — it must be a fairly stiff mixture. This should fill two sandwich tins. Bake for 30-40 minutes. Cut in half and spread with butter. This is best eaten hot.

# HOT CAKE
# TEISEN BOETH

4oz (125g) plain flour
2oz (50g) sugar
2 eggs
2oz (50g) butter or margarine
1 teaspoon baking powder

*Oven setting: Gas Mark 6 (400°F)*

Cream the butter and sugar, adding the flour, baking powder. Add the flour and beaten eggs alternately. Divide between two sandwich tins and bake in a hot oven for 12 to 15 minutes. Spread thickly with butter and sandwich the two halves together. Sprinkle the top with sugar. (Currants and raisins improve this cake if added.)

# HONEY CAKE

This is an ancient recipe dating originally from the time of the Crusades. It is commonly found nationwide, but the Welsh version includes cinnamon. It was especially popular during the eighteenth century.

*4oz (125g) honey*
*1 teaspoon cinnamon*
*4oz (125g) brown sugar*
*1 egg*
*½lb (225g) self raising flour*
*½ a teaspoon bicarbonate of soda*
*4oz (125g) butter or margarine*
*Caster sugar for dredging*
*A little milk*

*Oven setting: Gas Mark 6 (400°F)*

Sieve together the flour, cinnamon and bicarbonate of soda. Cream the butter and sugar. Separate the egg yolk from the white. Beat the yolk into the sugar and butter then add the honey gradually. Stir in the flour with some milk as required and blend all together lightly. Beat the egg white until stiff and fold into the mixture. Half fill small patty tins with the mixture; dredge the top of each with caster sugar and bake in a hot oven for 20 minutes. When cooked add some more sugar.

# APPLE BAKESTONE CAKE

The bakestone is among the most ancient of cooking utensils and its descendants include the griddle and frying pan. Either of these will cook this recipe adequately.

This cake is ideal for picnics — it can be eaten hot or cold.

*8oz (225g) shortcrust pastry*
*½oz (15g) butter*
*12oz (350g) cooking apples*
*2oz (50g) soft brown sugar*
*¼ teaspoon nutmeg*

Peel, core and slice the apples. Melt the butter in a pan and add the apples, sugar and nutmeg. Cover and stew gently, stirring frequently to prevent sticking for about 10 minutes. The apples should still be fairly firm, not pulpy.

Divide the pastry in two and roll each piece into a round of about 7 inches (18cm) across. Moisten the rim of one round and spread the apple on top to within about half an inch (1½cm) of the edge. Place the other round on top and press the edges gently together.

Brush the bakestone or frying pan with oil before heating. Lift the cake on to the griddle using a large spatula and cook for 10 minutes till brown. Turn it carefully, holding it between two large spatulas and cook for another 10 minutes on the other side.

Sprinkle with sugar and serve hot with cream or custard.

## PLUM TART
## TARTEN EIRIN

*Filling:*
*1lb (500g) plums, stoned and halved*
*4 small sliced apples*
*4oz (125g) sugar for sweetening and a little water*

*Pastry:*
*This is unusual in that it is spiced —*
*8oz (225g) plain flour*
*4oz (125g) margarine or half margarine, half lard*
*1/2oz sugar (15g)*
*1/4 teaspoon cinnamon*
*Pinch of mixed spice*

*Oven setting: Gas Mark 6 (400°F)*

Line a shallow tin or plate with half the pastry. Fill with fruit, cover with sugar and add a little water. Cover with the remaining pastry and bake for 45 minutes.

Fruit tarts of all sorts are popular in Wales. This one was chosen because of its specially delicious pastry.

Blackberry, blackberry and apple and winberry (whortleberries) are common variations.

## SHEARING CAKE
## CACEN GNEIFIO

This cake was generally eaten (often in the fields) at shearing time in the early part of the summer.

*1/2lb (225g) plain flour*
*6oz (175g) brown sugar*
*4oz (125g) butter*
*Rind of half a lemon*

*1 egg*
*¼ pint (150ml) milk*
*1 teaspoon baking powder*
*2 teaspoons carraway seeds*
*Grated nutmeg*

*Oven setting: Gas Mark 6 (400°F)*

Rub the butter into the flour, mix all the dry ingredients together and then stir in the milk and beaten egg. Bake in a greased cake tin lined with paper in a moderate oven for 1 hour.


## OVERNIGHT CAKE
## TEISEN DROS NOS

*½lb (225g) flour*
*4oz (125g) fat*
*4oz (125g) sugar*
*Mixed dry fruit*
*1 teaspoon cinnamon*
*1 teaspoon ginger*
*½ teaspoon bicarbonate of soda*
*1 tablespoon vinegar*
*Milk*

*Oven setting: Gas Mark 5 (375°F)*

Rub fat into flour and add rest of dry ingredients. Mix with milk and add the bicarbonate of soda with the vinegar and thoroughly stir. Leave batter overnight and bake next day in a lined and greased tin for about an hour.

# FARMHOUSE LARD CAKE

*1lb (450g) bread dough*
*8oz (225g) lard*
*4oz (125g) currants*
*2oz (50g) lemon peel*
*2oz (50g) sugar*

*Oven setting: Gas Mark 6 (400°F)*

Turn dough on to floured pastry board and roll out until it is about an inch thick; spread 2oz (50g) lard on the dough with 2oz (50g) of currants and 1oz (25g) peel. Repeat the rolling and larding until the dough has been rolled out four times.

Ensure that you do not press too heavily on the dough with the rolling pin. Bake in a well-greased tin in a moderate oven for about 1 hour. Serve cut into squares (hot or cold) with or without butter.

# FRUIT AND NUT CAKE
# TEISEN GNAU A FFRWYTHAU

*½lb (225g) self raising flour*
*3oz (75g) brown sugar*
*1 egg*
*½lb (225g) stoned dates*
*3oz (75g) shelled walnuts*
*¾ cup of boiling water*
*½ teaspoon bicarbonate of soda*
*½ teaspoon salt*

*Oven setting: Gas Mark 5 (375°F)*

Chop nuts and dates and add the bicarbonate and salt. Pour on the boiling water and leave to soak for two minutes. Add sugar, then the flour and lastly stir in the beaten egg.

Bake in a moderate oven for about 1 hour. This is delicious spread with butter or margarine.

## GREAT GRAN'S TEACAKE
## TEISEN DE HEN MAMGU

*½lb (225g) flour*
*1 teaspoon baking powder*
*3oz (75g) butter*
*3 tablespoons of milk*
*1 egg*
*3oz (75g) sugar*
*Pinch of salt*
*3 tablespoons of sherry*

*Oven setting — Gas Mark 5 (375°F)*

Rub the butter into the flour, add the sugar, baking powder and salt. Beat egg well and add milk and sherry. Stir this liquid into the other ingredients.

Bake in a shallow tin for about 20 minutes. Serve hot and well-buttered.

# RICE GRIDDLE CAKES
# TEISEN REIS GRADELL

*1 teacupful boiled rice*
*1 teacupful milk*
*1 teacupful flour*
*1 tablespoon of butter*
*1 teaspoon salt*
*2 teaspoons of baking powder*
*1 egg*

Mix together rice, melted butter, salt and the beaten egg. Sieve together the baking powder and flour, add to the mixture and stir well. Drop large tablespoonfuls on to hot greased bakestone or thick frying pan. Cook about four minutes each side.

These are irresistable when served hot with golden syrup.


# TEISEN LAP (1)


*1lb (500g) flour*
*4oz (125g) fat*
*4oz (125g) brown sugar*
*4oz (125g) mixed fruit*
*½ a teaspoon of bicarbonate of soda (dissolved in milk)*
*1 egg*
*½ pint (300ml) of buttermilk, single cream or alternatively sour milk*

Rub fat into flour, add sugar, fruit, spice; mix well together. Add the beaten egg and the milk and beat to a soft dough. Divide the dough and roll out to an inch in thickness; bake on a bakestone or hotplate; time about 15 minutes. When brown one side, turn them over.

# TEISEN LAP (2)

This old recipe would be best baked in a traditional Dutch oven before an open fire. Failing that a moderate oven is a good alternative.

*1lb (500g) flour*
*1 teaspoon baking powder*
*Pinch of salt*
*Grated nutmeg*
*4oz (125g) butter*
*4oz (125g) sugar*
*4oz (125g) dried sultanas and currants*
*3 eggs*
*½ pint (300ml) milk (again sour milk, if available, improves flavour)*

*Oven setting — Gas Mark 5 (375°F)*

Sieve flour, baking powder, salt and nutmeg. Rub in lightly the butter, add the sugar and fruit, whisk the eggs and add to mixture. Slowly add the milk mixing all the time with a wooden spoon. The consistency should be soft enough for the batter to drop from the spoon.

Spread the mixture thinly in a well-greased oblong tin and bake for 35 to 40 minutes.

## WELSH CAKES
## PICE AR Y MAEN

*8oz (250g) flour*
*½ teaspoon of baking powder*
*2oz (50g) margarine*
*2oz (50g) lard*
*3oz (75g) sugar*
*2oz (50g) currants*
*¼ teaspoon of mixed spice*
*Pinch of salt*
*1 egg*
*A little milk*

Rub fat into flour. Add dry ingredients, then egg and milk. Mix to a stiff paste — about the same as for short pastry. Roll out and cut into rounds to preferred thickness. Bake on bakestone, griddle or very thick frying pan.
(Special tip — a little golden syrup can make this recipe slightly more moist and delicious).

# CHRISTMAS CAKE
# TEISEN DDU NADOLIG

This is an old Cardiganshire recipe and is typical in that it includes some home brewed ale — but any pale ale will be fine. Do not use the whole bottle of pale ale though, since it would make the mixture rather too moist.

*1½lb (750g) flour*
*½lb (250g) butter or margarine*
*1lb (500g) castor sugar*
*4oz (125g) mixed peel*
*8oz (250g) currants*
*8oz (250g) raisins*
*4oz (125g) sweet almonds*
*½ a nutmeg grated*
*½oz (14g) of yeast*
*Mixerd spice if liked*
*Bottle of pale ale*
*Juice of half an orange and half a lemon*

*Oven setting — Gas Mark 5 (375°F)*

Rub the yeast into the flour, then rub in the fat, sugar, fruit and spices. Add the fruit juices and mix with the pale ale. Take care not to allow the mixture to become too soft. Bake in a moderate oven for about 3 hours. (Happy Christmas — Nadolig Llawen!)

# WELSH BREAD PUDDING

This was an economical dish utilising stale or not very fresh bread. You can use wholemeal or white loaves as preferred. Because it is nicer eaten cold, it was especially popular with the South Wales miners who would take it down the pits in their luncheon boxes.

*6-8 (or more) slices of bread including crusts*
*6oz (150g) or more fruit — sultanas, raisins, currants or a mixture of these*
*1 egg*
*2oz (50g) self raising flour*
*4oz (125g) soft brown sugar*
*2 teaspoons dried nutmeg*
*1 teaspoon cinnamon*
*½ to ¾ of a pint (300-325ml) milk*
*Grated eating apple (optional)*
*A little margarine to dot on the mixture during cooking*

*Oven setting — Gas Mark 2 (200°F)*

Allow the bread to soak in the milk for about 1 hour. Then add the egg, fruit, sugar, flour and spices. Mix very thoroughly until fairly smooth. Place in a well greased loaf tin, dot on some margarine, and bake in a slow oven for about 2 hours. This is tasty when hot, but nicer still when cold.

# STRAWBERRY RING

This is an old Pembrokeshire delicacy. The land there is ideal for the growth of soft fruits such as strawberries — the coastal warm winds protecting tender plants from frosts.

It is best to add the filling at the last minute to avoid the pastry becoming too soggy. Raspberries make a pleasant alternative to strawberries.

*2.5oz (65g) choux pastry*
*½ pint (300ml) double cream*
*3 tablespoons of icing sugar*
*1lb (500g) fresh strawberries*
*Icing sugar for dusting/almond flakes for decoration if liked*

*Oven setting — Gas Mark 7 (425°F)*

Using a forcing bag with a large plain nozzle, pipe the choux pastry into a ring about 1.5″ (20cm) across on to a greased baking tray. Bake in the centre of the oven for 30 minutes until golden brown.

When the choux ring is quite cool, but not cold, split it in half horizontally with a sharp knife.

For the filling, use a whisk and whip together the cream and icing sugar till light and fluffly. Spoon it into the bottom half of the ring. Arrange the fruit on top and around the sides of the heaped up cream. Place the choux lid on top and dust lightly with icing sugar.

# WELSH TOFFEE

This recipe is a traditional one from North Wales where Noson Gyflaith (Toffee Evening) was a major part of the Christmas celebrations. Families would invite friends to tea or supper and would gather around the fire to tell stories and make toffee.

When the toffee was being cooled, it would be put on to a greased hearthstone. Guests would then grease their hands and 'pull' the toffee into lovely golden spirals. Needless to say the First and Second World Wars saw the ending of this delightful pastime, but toffee making can still while away many a tedious winter evening.

*Sufficient for 1¾lb (800g)*
*4oz (125g) unsalted butter*
*1lb (450g) granulated sugar*
*2 tablespoons warm water*
*2 tablespoons white vinegar*
*4 tablespoons golden syrup or 2 tablespoons each of sugar and treacle*

Melt the butter in a large pan, stir in the sugar and take the pan from the heat.

Add the water, vinegar adn the syrup or syrup and treacle. Stir over a low heat till the sugar dissolves, taking care not to let the mixture boil. Then bring the mixture to boiling point. Boil steadily for about 15 to 20 minutes or until a little of the toffee put into a bowl of cold water will snap. The temperature (if you have a sweet thermometer) will be 152°C (305°F).

Pour toffee into a buttered rectangular tin measuring 11 by 7 (28 by 18cm).

Allow the toffee to cool. When it is beginning to set, mark it into squares. When quite cold, break the squares up and wrap each one in cellophane. It is best stored in airtight jars.

# DRESSINGS, SAUCES, PICKLES AND PRESERVES

Preserving fruits and pickles in Wales did not happen much before the eighteenth century when sugars, sauces and spices became more easily obtainable. The colonisation of India with its exotic chutneys led to a growing taste for these during the eighteenth century and the Victorian period. This period coincided with a rise in interest in garden cultivation and the introduction of more varied foods from America and the colonies.

## WELSH VEAL SAUCE
## SURYN CYFFAITH POETH

*6 lemons*
*2oz (50g) horseradish*
*1lb (450g) salt*
*6 cloves garlic*
*¼oz (7g) cloves*
*¼oz (7g) mace*
*¼oz (7g) nutmeg*
*¼oz (7g) cayenne*
*2oz (50g) mustard*
*4 pints (2.2l) malt vinegar*

Cut the lemons into slices of eighths and cover with salt. Cut the horseradish very finely, then place with the rest of the ingredients into a big jar that has a good fitting lid. Place the jar in a boiler of water (with the water coming to within 2 inches — 5cm — of the rim of the jar). Bring to the boil and boil for fifteen minutes. Stir the mixture every day for 6 weeks and keep the lid on. After 6 weeks, strain into small bottles and cork tightly. This very old recipe will keep for years and a little goes a very long way indeed.

# BEETROOT CHUTNEY

Beetroot, rather like leeks, grow abundantly in Wales' damp climate.

*2lb (900g) cooked beetroot*
*1lb (450g) cooking apples*
*1lb (450g) brown sugar*
*1 medium onion*
*1 lemon*
*½ pint (300ml) vinegar*

Chop apples and onion into small pieces. Add the vinegar. Bring to the boil in a large saucepan. Simmer till soft. Add sugar. Stir this in until dissolved. Add the lemon and chopped beetroot. Return this to the boil for 5 minutes. Place into warm jars. Cover when cold. This is delicious with Welsh cured ham or cold roast beef.

## SWEET APPLE CHUTNEY

*4lb (1.8kg) cooking apples*
*2lb (900g) small onions*
*2lb (900g) sugar*
*2 pints (1.1 litres) spiced vinegar*
*1oz (25g) turmeric powder*
*2oz (50g) cornflour*

Put the spiced vinegar into a preserving pan with the onions sliced thinly and cook for fifteen minutes. Add chopped apples and boil until the apples and onions are cooked. Add the sugar and turmeric powder and boil again for five minutes and thicken with the cornflour.

Pour into jars and seal down. This pickle is delicious served with Welsh Caerphilly cheese and fresh bread.

# TRADITIONAL SALAD DRESSING

*1 egg*
*1 tablespoon sugar*
*Dash of salt and pepper*
*1 teaspoon mustard*
*1 tablespoon melted butter*
*1 dessertspoon plain flour*
*1/2 teacup of milk*
*1/2 teacup vinegar*
*1/2 teacup warm water*

Mix egg, sugar, salt and pepper together. Add the mustard and flour till it becomes a nice smooth paste. Then add the melted butter, milk, water and finally the vinegar.

Cook over a low heat until as thick as cream, but do not boil. Keep this in a jar in the refrigerator for up to one week.


# GOOSEBERRY MINT JELLY

Some of Wales' land is poor and ill-drained. Nevertheless, the hardy gooseberry grows well enough under such conditions and was a popular preserve.

*2lb (900g) green gooseberries (cleaned and topped and tailed)*
*6 stalks of fresh mint*
*1lb (450g) sugar per pint of liquid*

Place the gooseberries in a preserving pan, just cover with cold water and cook until soft. Strain carefully and to each pint of liquid add 1lb (450g) of sugar. Pour back into the preserving pan together with the mint tied into a bundle. Heat gently till the sugar is melted, then boil until it 'gels'. Then remove the mint, pour into glass jars and seal.

# WELSH HOME MADE WINES AND BEVERAGES

Welsh ale houses were well established before the Norman invasion of 1066. Their ale was then made of fermented grain and was the most common drink — so adults would drink strong twice-brewed ales, while children would enjoy weaker 'small ale' — later 'small beer'. Ale made of hops did not occur until the fifteenth century when the hop plant reached this country from what is now the Netherlands. This was popular because it had better keeping qualities than the old fashioned drink.

Though wines were produced in Wales and other parts of the country after the Roman fashion, it was mainly in the monastic houses. Only in the eighteenth century when sugar became cheap and plentiful did the making of country wines become widespread.

# BLACKBERRY WINE
# GWIN MWYAR DUON

*6lb (2.7kg) blackberries*
*4lb (1.8kg) white sugar*
*8 pints (4.4 litres) boiling water*
*½oz (15g) yeast*

Pour the boiling water on to the blackberries. Stir well, night and morning for two days. Strain. Dissolve the sugar in the liquid and add the yeast. Stir well.

Pour the sweetened yeasted liquid into a clean jar or bottle (depending on quantity) until it is filled to the top. Retain any surplus in a bottle for topping up the water container during fermentation. Stand the jar or bottle on a tray in a warm room. Fermentation soon begins and froth will pour over the side of the container. Fill up again from the surplus bottle until a froth no longer forms. Insert a cork into the container, loosely at first, but when the fermentation is over and no bubbles of gas are seen, then cork tightly. If you want a really clear wine, it should be racked occasionally — that is, pour the clear wine from the old bottles into clean ones, keeping the yeast deposit to re-clear in the old bottles. Keep the wine for a minimum of six months before sampling. £

Please note £ to £ is the traditional Welsh method of wine making in all cases.

## WHEAT OR POTATO WINE
## GWIN GWENITH NEU WIN TATWS

*2lb (900g) old potatoes, unpeeled, sliced small*
*2lb (900g) raisins, split*
*1lb (450g) washed wheat*
*4lb (1.8kg) demerara sugar*
*4 pints (2.2 litres) boiling water*
*1oz (25g) yeast*

Pour the boiling water on to the other ingredients and stir well. When cool, add the yeast and cover for fourteen days, stirring reularly, night and morning. Strain, then proceed as from £ to £ above. This should be kept for at least twelvemonths.


## WELSH ELDERBERRY WINE
## GWIN YSGAW

*7lb (3.2kg) elderberries stalked and stripped*
*3lb (1.4kg) sugar (traditionally loaf sugar would be used)*
*1lb (450g) seedless raisins*
*½oz (15g) yeast*
*6 cloves*
*24 pints boiling water*

Place berries in a large vessel and cover with the boiling water. Leave to stand for 24 hours. Mash the fruit and strain through a jelly-bag. Put in a preserving pan adding the sugar, ginger, raisins and cloves. Boil slowly for one hour, skimming all the time. Let the liquid cool and add the yeast. Pour into an earthenware vessel and leave to ferment for two weeks. Bottle and cork and let the wine stand for at least three months.

## ELDERFLOWER WINE
## GWIN BLODYN YSGAW

*1 pint (600ml) flowers only with no green stalks*
*3lb (1.4kg) sugar*
*3 lemons*
*8 pints (4.4 litres) cold water*

Put all these ingredients in a pan, cover with a cloth and stand for a fortnight, stirring every day. Then proceed from £ to £ as above.

## PARSLEY WINE

*1lb (450g) parsley — leaves but not stalks*
*2 oranges*
*2 lemons*
*4lb (1.8kg) demerara sugar*
*8 pints (4.4 litres) water*
*Yeast (½oz (15g) to the gallon)*

Put the parsley in a muslin bag with the lemon and orange rinds. Pour the water over it and bring to the boil. Simmer for half an hour. Squeeze the bag and remove from the pan. Add the sugar — 4lb (1.8kg) to the gallon (4.4 litres) and the fruit juices. When the mixture has cooled, add the yeast (½oz (15g) to the gallon — 4.4 litres) and proceed from £ to £ as before.

# RHUBARB WINE

*5lb (2.25kg) rhubarb*
*4lb (1.8kg) sugar*
*Juice of 2 lemons*
*1lb (450g) raisins*
*8 pints (4.4 litres) water*

Place the chopped rhubarb, unpeeled, into a pan and add the water. Allow to stand for a week to soften. Strain and add the sugar, juice and raisins. If a very clear wine is required add a quarter of an ounce (7g) of isinglass dissolved in a little warm water. Stir every day and when it ceases to 'work' bottle it, but do not cork tightly til the 'hissing' has stopped.

# NETTLE AND BURDOCK DRINK

*4 pints (2.2 litres) nettles (gathered carefully using gloves!)*
*2oz (50g) hops*
*2oz (50g) burdock*
*12 pints (6.6 litres) water*
*2lb (900g) sugar*
*1 lemon*
*2oz (50g) yeast*

Boil the nettles, hops and burdock slowly for half an hour. Strain, add sugar and sliced lemon. Leave til luke-warm. Place the yeast, spread on round of toasted bread, on top of the brew. Leave for 12 hours. Bottle and make airtight. Can be drunk after 12 hours. This is a refreshing light drink which is ideal for hot summer afternoons.

# PUMPKIN WINE
# GWIN PWMPEN

Take a large pumpkin and remove the seeds and pulp. Place the pumpkin in a large jar or suitable vessel.

Fill the cavity with granulated sugar, cover with a cloth and stand in a warm place. Each day add more sugar until the pumpkin has completely dissolved. Then strain the liquor, add the juice of two lemons and for each 2 pints (1.1 litres) add a quarter of a pint (200ml) rum. Pour into bottle immediately and cork tightly.

Keep this for six months before enjoying.


# HERB BEER
# DIOD DAIL

*About a dozen nettle tops*
*1oz (25g) dandelion leaves*
*1oz (25g) root ginger*
*1lb (450g) demerara sugar*
*½oz (15g) yeast*

This recipe was traditionally considered to be helpful in alleviating arthritis and asthma.

Tie the bruised ginger in muslin and boil with herbs in 8 pints (4.4 litres) of cold water for about half an hour. Strain on to the sugar and stir well. When lukewarm put in the yeast floating on a piece of toast. Stand overnight and bottle the next day. Cork tightly. This light and refreshing drink is ready within two or three days. This is superb for a summer picnic. In days gone by it was a popular standby for thirsty Welsh mine and farm workers.

## WELSH GINGER BEER
## DIOD SINSIR

Take a 10 pint (5.5 litres) saucepan half-filled with dandelions and nettles in equal proportions, together with two sticks of rhubarb and four sticks of ginger previously pounded.

Fill up with cold water. Boil all the ingredients together for about fifteen minutes together with a handful of blackcurrant leaves. Then strain and add 1lb (450g) of white sugar to the liquid. Stir and add eight pints (4.5 litres) of cold water.

When this mixture is lukewarm, mix one ounce (25g) of yeast in a cup of the liquid and add it to the remainder. Leave overnight. In the morning skim off the yeast and bottle the liquid, but do not cork too tightly at first.


## SMALL BEER
## CWRW BACH

This is another tonic drink — thought to provide energy and strength. Nettles, surprisingly are a good source of vitamin C and iron.

Boil together for half an hour 10 pints (5.5 litres) water, 3 dozen dandelions, 3 dozen nettles, 6 sticks of pounded ginger, 3 sticks rhubarb, some blackcurrant tops and 2 handfuls of hops.

Strain and add 1lb (450g) demerara sugar; stir and add 6 pints (3.4 litres) cold water; when lukewarm sprinkle 1oz (25g) yeast over the surface.

Leave overnight, then skim and bottle. This can be drunk within a few days.

## APPLE WINE
## GWIN AFALAU

*(A good windfall recipe)*
*8 pints (4.5 litres) apples*
*8 pints (4.5 litres) boiling water*
*2 lemons*
*Piece of bruised ginger*
*A few cloves*
*Sugar*

Crush apples, pour over boiling water, cover with a cloth and leave for a fortnight, squeezing daily. Strain, add cloves and ginger and allow half a pound (225g) sugar to each pint (600ml) of liquor. Add lemon juice, stir well until the sugar has dissolved. Leave to stand till a scum has formed on the surface. Skim, pour into bottles, and tie corks down securely.

Leave about 6 months before sampling.